Mel Bay Presents

A CELTIC ❦ TINWHIS
CHRISTMAS

**Arranged and edited
by James Tanguay**

CW00405939

index of tunes

wassail ! wassail !

ancient english

The Wexford Carol

irish

we wish you a merry christmas

english

sans day carol

cornish

all you that in this house

english

child in the manger

scottish

christmas day is come

irish

the darkest midnight in december

Irish

the furry day carol

cornish

13

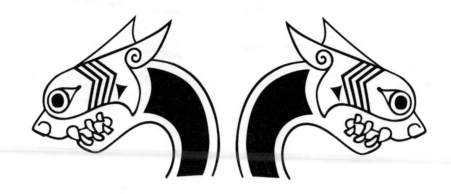

christmas is coming

a three part round
each player begins when the preceeding player reaches the second line. he then repeats and
stops at the hold when the first player reaches the end of the tune for the third time.

this new christmas carol

cornish

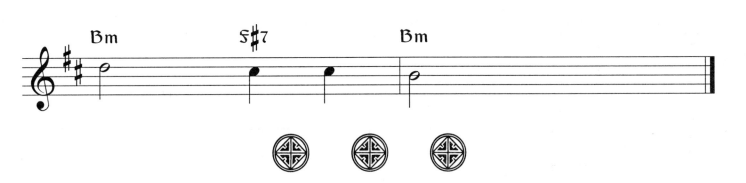

here we come awassailing

english

righteous joseph

cornish

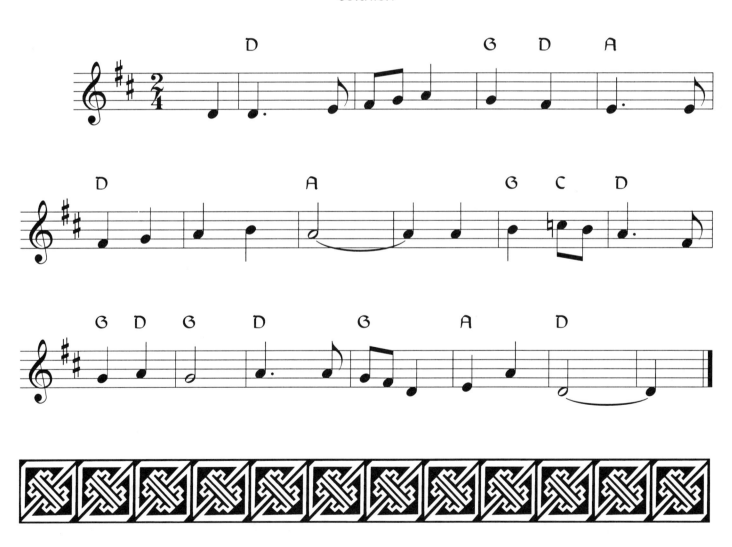

joy to the world

english

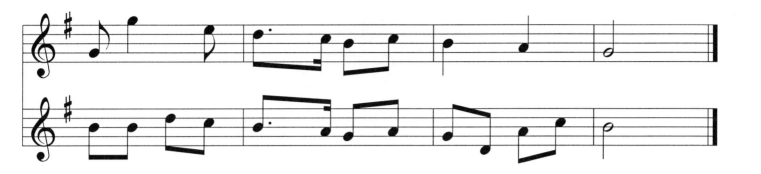

gloucestershire wassail

english

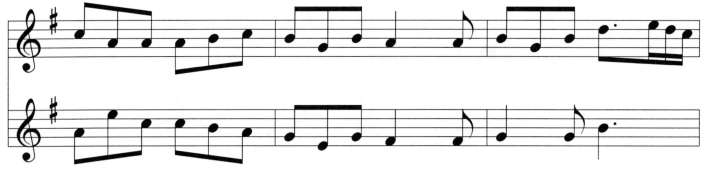

the eeny round

from the eenies

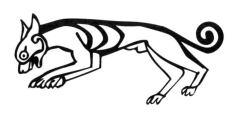

a two part round

player 1 repeats the tune and stops at the hold after the number 2. player 2 begins when player 1 reaches the number 2 for the first time. he then repeats and stops at the hold after the number 1.

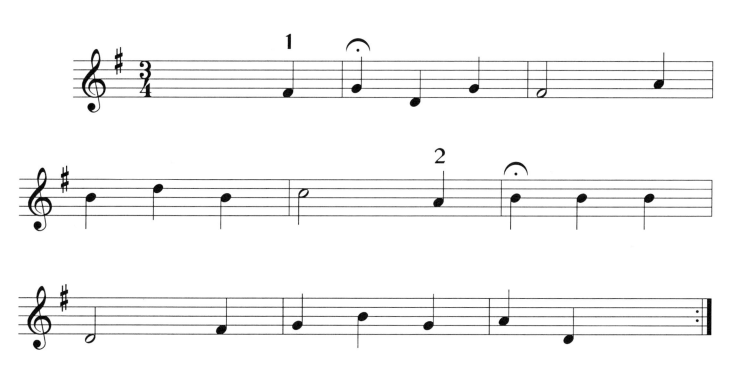

joseph and gentle mary

irish

while shepherds watched

english

deck the halls

welsh

I saw three ships asailing in

english

the coventry carol

english

the holly and the ivy girl

Irish

the christ child's lullaby

hebridian

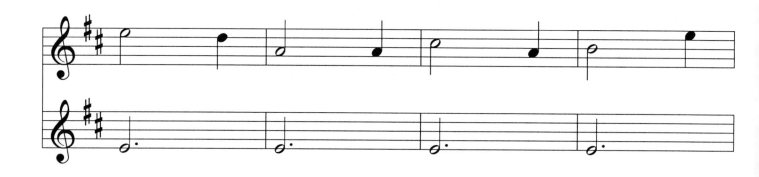

god rest ye merry gentlemen

english

peace and joy
merry christmas to all